Digital Pr

Josef Reisz

This Sales Pocket Guide is a concise, easy-to-read book that will help you get more business.

The Complete Digital Prospecting Guide for Lead Generation and Marketing Success: How to Find and Prospect Hi-ROI Sales Leads and Marketing Clients with LinkedIn and Social Media

This book is for sales leaders and sales people in account-based marketing sales organisations, sharing the most effective ways for digital prospecting on LinkedIn. The top methods are outlined, including getting endorsements from prospects, collecting names in one central location, setting up alerts for when prospects are interested, and building strong relationships with prospects leading to meaningful sales conversations, and ultimately convert into sales.

1

About Josef Reisz

Josef Reisz is a CEO with over 25 years of experience in the development of new markets, strategic planning and implementation.

Josef has been on both sides of the table; as an Entrepreneur, he started out by founding six successful companies, such as VU Capital, JRC Strategic Business Advisory and, most recently, HoneyComb Agency.

He also has extensive experience working for Fortune 500 corporations as well as smaller privately-owned businesses - holding various roles such as Head of Sales, Marketing and eCommerce.

Josef Reisz is a serial entrepreneur with an impressive track record. He has had experience in various roles on the C- and Board level held positions as Head of Sales, Head of Marketing, Head of Ecommerce, CEO, Non-Exec and Advisory Board member.

Josef has written five books on topics ranging from personal growth to business success. His writings have helped countless people build better lives while growing their respective brands or companies.

About HoneyComb

At HoneyComb, we help Sales Organisations Transform Into Well-Oiled And Inspired POWERHOUSES by Strategic And Tactical Design.

HOLISTIC STRATEGY DESIGN
Have our team of experts with 25 years experience design and implement a holistic business growth strategy across all your organisation's departments. A unified powerhouse.

CORPORATE SALES TRAINING
In-Depth training for your sales team enables them to hit their targets, stay motivated and incentivised, close more deals and generate more, predictable revenue for your organisation

TAILORED CONTENT CRAFTSMANSHIP
A team of wordsmiths crafting fresh, high quality content at scale and publish it on all your channels with your own unique brand voice.

www.HoneyCombAgency.co.uk

THE SALES TRANSFORMATION COMPANY

HONEYCOMB

Introduction   **6**

The 3 Stages   **8**

Digital Prospecting Strategy   **12**

Identify Target Accounts   12

Identify Decision Makers   14

Identify Influencers   16

Do your Research   17

Activate your Network   18

Finding relevant, common connections   20

Find Your Undervalued Leads   21

Changing Jobs? Great!   22

Add value within social selling   24

Build your Pipeline   26

A Stellar LinkedIn Profile   28

Key Takeaways   30

Account Entry Campaign   31

Real Life Example   34

Your First Touch Point with Prospects   36

Follow Up   38

Know Your Endgame   40

Your Daily Social Selling Routine   41

For Executives and Sales Leaders   **43**

How to Measure Social Selling   44

Social Selling Definition   45

Social Selling KPIs for Sales Leaders   46

Irrelevant, traditional KPIs   47

A New Set of KPIs   48

Measuring   50

Technology   51

Social CRM   52

Quantifiable Insights for Sales Leaders   54

Conclusion   55

Conclusion   **60**

Introduction

As the social media landscape changes, social selling is becoming increasingly important as a tool for companies looking to grow their business.

The problem with social selling is that it takes a different mindset, attitude and strategy. You need know-how about how social selling works before you can get results quickly or easily.

Skeptics might say that it's too easy to get burned by these digital tools.

They would say that the average person doesn't want to be bothered with this hard-sell approach, and they're too busy to care about someone they've never met telling them about something they don't need or want.

The book discusses a variety of approaches to LinkedIn prospecting, including through first-party platforms, third-party platforms and first-party webpages.

The other major thing I'll mention is that this book has a heavy focus on account-based marketing.

The book also includes examples of best practices from the author's experience as a salesperson as well as other industry experts.

Are you a sales leader who are looking for new sales people to maintain customer relationships, or a salesperson looking to 'up' your game?

Then this book is for you!

The 3 Stages

The three stages of networking on LinkedIn.

I going to bust a myth now: It's really simple. I mean, REALLY simple. Not easy, though. But simple. Digital prospecting is on the rise. The power in the marketplace has shifted noticeably from the Seller side to the Buyer side. Buyers today are inundated with an overload of information.

How can you break through this clutter and establish yourself and your solution as thought leaders?

Easy: By following simple rules outlined in this book.

On the surface, these are the 3 simple steps:

> *1) Getting your profile right*
>
> *2) Ensuring you're visible*
>
> *3) Engaging with your connections through great content, comments or asking questions.*

Digital prospecting has been proven to be a better ROI than email or phone prospecting for B2B companies.

Social selling has been replacing the traditional salesman approach with a value-focused individual who constantly monitors their networks for prospects.

Digital prospecting is an art form in itself, just as sales. You won't master it until you apply it and learn from your mistakes. The top social selling software on the market is LinkedIn Sales Navigator and social prospecting tools such as: Rapportive, Find and Know, Buzzstream.

Marketing has become more complex than ever before - with social media platforms constantly evolving and prospects becoming more busy and harder to reach

Social selling helps you create authenticity with your connections. The goal of social selling is not to sell, it's to provide value first then ask for a favour or referral later.

But how do you find those buyers? And just as importantly, how do you approach them? How can social selling help give insight into what makes up a successful social seller?

Digital prospecting on LinkedIn can be used by salespeople in any industry, however social selling is either misunderstood or misaligned.

Social selling can help you be more aware of the social space and where your potential prospects are spending time online. This allows salespeople to put themselves on the map as a social influencer in their industry

The first step of digital prospecting with social media is to find your target audience, then determine which social networks they use most often so that you can build your social presence there

The goal of social prospecting is not only to establish yourself as an authority but connect with decision makers who will ultimately become customers, all before traditional methods come into play.

Digital prospecting opens up new ways for prospects to have meaningful conversations with you. A key component of social networking is engagement.

Consider social media as a way of establishing thought leadership and social context around your brand, service or product.

And it's not just social selling - there are many benefits of social networking for Salespeople that include staying relevant, creating visibility, building trust, earning authority and insight into your industry

Because of the changing nature of social media platforms, social prospecting is more complex than ever before. Social networking has become an integral part of B2B marketing plans - with LinkedIn becoming one of the most powerful social networks to build your target audience and find potential prospects online.

Content curation allows you to filter through information quickly in order to identify what may be relevant for you to read about when it comes to digital prospect

Digital Prospecting Strategy

Identify Target Accounts

In order to identify the companies that your prospects want to target you should apply certain factors:

1. *Industry*

2. *Location*

3. *Annual Revenue*

4. *Headcount*

5. *Growth Rate*

6. *Ethics & Values*

This will help you figure out what industries and companies we want to focus on first.

Once you have your target accounts, social selling requires that you engage with the right people within these organisations. These are usually high-level executives involved in making purchase decisions. It is not about how many connections you have but who they are

Create a list of your top 5-10 prospects, prioritise them in order of most likely to buy. Using an account-based marketing approach helps here as you can see which companies are in each person's network, this will give you an idea on which companies they work at and will be more likely to respond to messages sent through social media.

Identify Decision Makers

For each target account that you have identified on LinkedIn Sales Navigator, you want to look for 3-5 decision makers on different executive- and responsibilities levels. For example:

1. *Head of Sales*

2. *Head of Marketing*

3. *Head of IT*

4. *Chief Digital Officer*

5. *Chief Operating Officer*

6. *Sales Manager*

7. *Marketing Executive*

8. *and so on*

Why is it important to identify more than one decision maker in your target accounts? Because this will help you to not only address the right person at your target accounts, but also gives you the opportunity to address several people which are of equal or different rank.

They might not be involved in the decision making process but can act as your personal influencer within the target company, working alongside you - as a social seller - to help you make such a strong case that their higher up will become as enthusiastic as they are about your product.

The more you know who's at the helm of each target account, the clearer it becomes how to social-sell them through your social selling strategy.

At the end of this stage, you'll have B2B LinkedIn social selling search filters and prospecting lists with names and positions of decision makers so social selling can be used to full potential at each target company.

Identify Influencers

What is an influencer within an organisation? An influencer is a person within your target account that has no purchasing power but can influence the decision making process and the ultimate decision makers.

Why is it important to engage with influencers as well as high-level decision makers? Simple, you want to leverage your standing within your target account as much as you can.

Hence, you need someone 'on your side' who understands your solution and advocates for it. I.e. Your influencer within your target account.

When you engage with your social selling accounts, identify who the influencers are. Once identified, initiate contact using social selling best practices .

Do your Research

The internet is a great place to research the target account. By searching social media usernames or company names within social networks such as Twitter, Facebook and LinkedIn it becomes very easy to find profiles that belong to people in your target account.

It's also possible to use Google Search to find profiles belonging to people at your target account. When you have found their social network profile(s), investigate further by checking out what they're talking about and who they're engaging with on social media. This will help you establish how 'special' they are in terms of influence inside your prospect organisation.

Activate your Network

LinkedIn is a social network that enables you not only to search on first-, last name or company name for potential unknown connections that you may have on LinkedIn, but also to find existing alumni of yours from universities and colleges.

Searching for alumni on LinkedIn can be very efficient especially when targeting large companies because often times they consist out of more than one division with its own different employees within these divisions.

Just imagine, you are about to start with a new project for one of the divisions, alumni from your previous job or even studies could be vital assets that you didn't know were there. Put your connections to good use and ask for a warm introduction

A connection on LinkedIn doesn't necessarily mean that you know someone so it's not mandatory to message them about the cold call. However, almost everyone of us has established some kind of relationship with at least one of our connections on LinkedIn. This is why it's always advised to ask your contacts if they could help you out by providing a warm introduction.

Doing this can save you hours of research because this way an employee will do most of the work within seconds and all you need to do is pick up the phone and start talking.

Finding relevant, common connections

LinkedIn has a great feature: It shows you how you are connected to your prospect. Maybe through a common contact, a group, a topic, etc. Utilise these connections to get your foot in the door with your prospect.

Another great social selling strategy on LinkedIn is to search for experts or influencers in your industry that are connected with one of your prospects.

You can then directly message them and ask them if they know someone within the same company that you're targeting. If you're lucky, this social selling strategy could land you an introduction with the decision maker at your target account!

Also, do not underestimate the connective power of LinkedIn groups. Having a group in common could be a great opener for a conversation.

Find Your Undervalued Leads

LinkedIn offers some great functionalities that will help you to identify undervalued leads. For example, the 'Who's viewed your profile' feature. It shows you who visited your profile, which companies they are from, which sectors and so on.

This is important because it gives you an indication of who might actually be interested in what you have to offer - especially with executive level people.

The more they visit your profile, the more likely they are willing to engage with you initially. It's also a good indicator that they may even know about your product or service already which makes the conversation easier.

Changing Jobs? Great!

LinkedIn has this great feature that it allows you to notify your whole network about your new job. Well, isn't that something!

I have used this feature so many times to start conversations with contacts I had not engaged with in a long time.

A new position is also a new opportunity for you to connect with your existing network. Not only will they see that you are starting a new position. They will most likely send you a congratulation message. BOOM. Perfect! Let's hit reply, say Thank you and ask a cheeky "Hey, what are you up to these days? How's it going at COMPANY? What are your plans for TRIGGER EVENT (or your VALUE PROPOSITION)?"

See, everything is at your fingertips - literally - to start engaging with your existing network and have meaningful conversations.

Will it always work? No. Not everyone in your network might have an active project where your solution could fit in. But…if you don't ask, you don't get.

Add value within social selling

So now you have found some connections through social selling on LinkedIn, but what do you do next? Well, it depends per individual relationship what approach will work best for them, but in general adding value is at the core of social selling. As an account-based marketing sales leader or sales person, adding value is a key skill.

You have to know how and when you can add value for the people you want to connect with on social selling sites, such as LinkedIn. Of course, social selling is a long-term strategy, so adding value does not mean spamming people all the time or just sharing your own content - that's just being annoying!

In order to be able to add value within social selling, first identify some areas where your target prospects would benefit from additional information , insight or knowledge .

In other words: what problems do they have? What questions do they need answered? How could their business grow and evolve by taking advantage of new information and insights?

Second, find ways in which you can provide them with this additional information ,insight or knowledge. This might be through social selling yourself, giving them a link to an article you read somewhere, recommending a book they could read about their industry topic of interest...

In the end social selling is all about adding value and getting added value in return. You have to know which approach will work best for each individual connection that you make before going out there and social selling on LinkedIn.

It's important not to spam people with your own content, but provide them with information which they lack at the moment - just like what you do in account-based marketing!

Build your Pipeline

Once you've completed these step, it's time to start building up your pipeline by making use of social selling. It's time to social sell! When social selling is done properly, it will be worth gold because of its high ROI on social media - the social media world is full of potential customers who are actively looking for new information about topics they're interested in.

LinkedIn social selling gets them into your company's industry, research and thought leadership content gets them even closer to becoming a client that eventually becomes part of your focused target account list.

At this stage, you'll have identified several decision makers at each target account while building up your pipeline with social selling so you can influence the right person at the right time.

You've also activated your network on LinkedIn by finding alumni from universities or colleges so you have an extended network of professionals who might be willing to help you with social selling.

At this point, social selling has become a process and is an integral part of the sales cycle that you're using for account-based marketing and sales development.

You'll need several tools to social sell:

- *A social media listening tool like Brand24 to monitor what's being said about your product or service;*

- *LinkedIn Sales Navigator to research leads; Rapportive to link social profiles with email addresses (so you know who you're social selling);*

- *Hootsuite or SproutSocial to schedule social content;*

- *Notify by Buffer or Parse.ly to follow up on links within social posts and emails .*

A Stellar LinkedIn Profile

Your LinkedIn profile must be stellar, professional and engaging. Make sure that you have an enticing and interest-piquing LinkedIn profile with a great profile image, a cover photo and description.

Ideally, you are posting regularly, every day, on LinkedIn providing valuable and irresistible industry-related and relevant information.

LinkedIn is the leading B2B social network for professionals, and it's where social sellers do their work. LinkedIn profiles are a key part of your social selling strategy, as they're how you'll identify prospects and connect with them on this platform.

A stellar LinkedIn profile can set you apart from other salespeople trying to do the same thing - so let's learn how to create one!

It is of utmost importance to have a professional LinkedIn profile, personally and for your company. Your LinkedIn profile is often the first impression you make on a prospective client or customer, so it should be professional in every way

Your LinkedIn profile is often the first thing that a prospect will see when considering your services or products - and if they aren't wowed by what you have to offer right away, chances are good that they're gone.

That is why having a professional LinkedIn profile is so important.

Your social selling strategy is most effective when you can be found on LinkedIn and other social media sites such as Facebook, Twitter and Instagram.

Wherever your prospects are. It will take trust and investment in social selling for companies to see value in social selling platforms like LinkedIn.

Naturally, building your digital presence on social media and social selling platforms such as LinkedIn is an integral part of your social selling strategy.

How can you expect to be five steps ahead of your competition if you're not even on social media?

Key Takeaways

A stellar LinkedIn profile is where social sellers do their work. To stand out from other salespeople, make sure that your LinkedIn profile is professional and engaging.

By posting regularly on social selling platforms like LinkedIn, you can generate leads and trust more quickly than traditional social selling methods.

Have a professional photograph taken, an eye-catching cover image, an easy-to-read and engaging description and job title.

Make sure that you post valuable, engaging and educating content relevant to your solution and target audience.

Account Entry Campaign

On average, a sales person needs 9 touch points - at least - to get a response from a prospect that eventually leads to a scheduled meeting or phone call.

Shockingly, most sales reps give up after 3 attempts. A huge lost opportunity.

Your account entry campaign needs to be planned and strategised before your launch it. Surprisingly, only a small number of companies have a defined account entry strategies.

First thing to do is develop a social selling strategy:

What social networks does your target use most? What social networks will you use most?

Where do the most activity happens? How can you spend most time there so that it provides the most value for your business? What social selling skills do my reps need before they start prospecting on social media ?

Start by going through all social channels and mapping out your targets - both decision makers and influencers - as well as their current conversation topics.

To get more precise, your Account Entry Strategy is comprised of at least 9 touch points per prospect. Meaning, if you have 5 prospects in one account, you will have 45 touch points in total in your plan.

Example

1. *LinkedIn Invite*

2. *LinkedIn Message*

3. *Post Engagement*

4. *Phone Call attempt 1 / Leave Voice Message*

5. *Send Email 1*

6. *LinkedIn Engagement*

7. *Phone Call Attempt 2 / Leave Voice Message*

8. *Send Email 2 / LinkedIn Message*

9. *Twitter Engagement*

10. *LinkedIn Message*

I focus LinkedIn as it is the best way I have found to connect and engage with prospects. Of course, if your prospect is more active on Twitter, go on Twitter and engage there!

Be social, be engaging, be of value. It doesn't matter where you build a relationship with your prospect. As long as you make it happen.

Let me share a real life example from my personal professional life on the next page.

Real Life Example

A while ago, I was asked to get access to a decision maker in a large, multi-national corporation. Here are my exact steps:

1. *Identified the account*

2. *Identified 3 decision makers*

3. *Researched online*

4. *Found an interview with the decision makers on YouTube*

5. *Looked them up on LinkedIn*

6. *Sent invite*

7. *Added note referring to the interview*

8. *One of the decision makers accepted my invite straight away*

9. *Sent LinkedIn message immediately after invite accepted*

10. *Ping-pong messages with decision maker*

11. *Scheduled Call with him in 2 week's time (done within 30 minutes of our initial LinkedIn messages)*

12. *Prepared for the call*

13. *Conducted the call*

14. *Closed the deal*

If your prospect still does not respond to your outreach, it is now time to up the game. As you have already learned by now, we do not rely on only one prospect per account.

Our aim is to identify at 3, ideally 5. So when one prospect turns out to be a 'Black Hole', you can approach the other 4.

Reach out to them. You already know who they are, what you could offer them and what they need from the company. And the best part is, these prospects have an interest in working with you as there is social proof through a mutual connection.

Your First Touch Point with Prospects

Your first touch point after identifying potential prospects is your LinkedIn invite. Now, much has been said about whether to send a note alongside your invite. At HoneyComb, we have tested various ways and we can now say: It does not matter. We have received the same amount of 'Invite accepted' with or without an accompanying note.

Having said that, depending on your LinkedIn profile and your experience, you might want to add a note, explaining the reasons as to why you want to connect. As social selling is not only about prospecting, it might be viewed as spam if you do not send any context. Of course, depending on the industry you are in, note size and word count will differ.

Pro Tip:

Some users automatically click 'Accept' when they receive a request with no note. I have tested it personally, with HoneyComb and our clients. I've come to the conclusion that you don't necessarily need an accompanying note with an invite. If you have a professional profile that's relevant to your prospect, you're in.

If you want to test it in an A/B test (with and without a note), here's a simple, yet highly effective note you can try:

Hi [FIRST NAME], Looking to connect and discuss [SECTOR]-related topics with you. Best, [MY NAME]

You might also want to refer to a Trigger Event, such as:

Hi [FIRST NAME], Saw your recent post [or presentation] on [TOPIC]. Looking to connect and discuss further. Best, [MY NAME]

These two strategies have helped me grow my network tremendously quick with the right high-level decision makers.

Remember that executives don't have time - or don't want to take time - to read a 'novel'. Keep it short, simple and straight to the point.

Follow Up

As the saying goes: The money is in the Follow Up.

You are not like the majority of the sales people who give up after 3 attempts. Be the exception! Make sure you have a solid follow up strategy as outlined in the account entry campaign.

How long it takes to get a response from a social prospect is key in determining a social selling approach.

After 3 follow ups, your social prospect will be feeling you nagging at them and that's when things can go bad. Don't take unnecessary risks if they have not responded after the third time. Move on! Put a follow up reminder in your calendar in 4 weeks or 6 weeks. Then get back to them.

Always remember:
There are plenty of social prospects out there waiting for you...

I recommend using this strategy:

- *1st attempt, social prospect responds or doesn't respond;*

- *2nd attempt, social prospect responds or doesn't respond;*

- *3rd attempt, social prospect does not respond;*

- *4th attempt (if applicable), call/email social prospect;*

- *5th+ attempts (if necessary), move on and leave alone for a week or two (or even longer).*

Giving a prospect time and space is essential if you don't want to be perceived as pushy or sales-y.

Remember that you have at 4 other decision makers identified and you can 'play the game' with them now and come back to your first prospect if and when needed.

Also, as part of your account entry outreach, you will have more than just LinkedIn to get in touch with your prospect. Use phone, email, text (when appropriate) in your mix. And change your message with each medium.

Know Your Endgame

What's your endgame? Do you know? You should. What outcome are you looking to achieve by applying and implementing social selling and digital prospecting into your sales strategy?

1. *Pique interest*

2. *Book a call or meeting*

3. *Close the lead*

Knowing your endgame helps you to strategise and work towards a goal. All 3 points above are essential if your endgame is to generate more revenue to your bottom-line.

Each step is a success and needs to be measured and tracked. Make social selling and digital prospecting work for you by knowing your endgame.

Your Daily Social Selling Routine

It is important to have a daily routine to share relevant and valuable content, engage with your prospects and make your efforts 'sticky-sweet' - Btw, follow HoneyComb's hashtag #StickySweetSales on LinkedIn. Thank you :)

1. *LinkedIn (Sales Navigator)*

2. *Message new connections with a Thank you note*

3. *Check new messages*

4. *Check for relevant company updates*

5. *Check 'Saved Leads' updates*

6. *Check saved searches for new leads/ accounts*

7. *CRM*

8. *Check email opens / clicks*

9. *Check new website visitors, i.e. via LeadInfo*

10. *Check new registrations on your lead magnets*

11. *Email*

12. *Check who replied*

13. *Send Emails to prospects as part of your 'Account Entry Campaign'*

14. *Follow Up*

15. *I said it before and I'll say it again: Your Money is in the Follow Up*

16. *Research Trigger Evens*

On a daily basis, go on Google, your prospect's website, LinkedIn, Twitter, YouTube and look for significant Trigger Events relevant to your campaign.

Use tools such as Craft to get insights on your target company, key contacts and their competitors.

Use these Trigger Events to initiate a conversation, or at least a touch point. Remember, if your prospect does not respond, it does count as a touch point, nevertheless.

For Executives and Sales Leaders

What's the social selling strategy for your company?

How can social selling be used in an account-based marketing (ABM) sales organisation?

What results are you looking to achieve by using social selling and digital prospecting?

Who should be focusing on social selling? Who should be focused on lead generation with LinkedIn, social media, etc.?

How to Measure Social Selling

How can you measure Social Selling? Social selling is a way of using social media to generate leads and drive sales. Social Selling is one of the fastest growing trends in B2B marketing, but measuring success can be difficult for companies that are still trying to figure out how it works.

This guide will help you understand what your KPIs should be tracking, as well as provide some insight into how other organisations are measuring Social Selling's impact on revenue generation. Social selling is a way of using social media to generate leads and drive sales.

Social Selling is one of the fastest growing trends in B&B marketing, but measuring success can be difficult for companies that are still trying to figure out how it works.

This guide will help you understand what your KPIs should be tracking, as well as provide some insight into how other organisations are measuring Social Selling's impact on revenue generation. Social selling is a way of using social media to generate

Social Selling Definition

A quick recap:

Social selling refers to leveraging social networking websites, such as LinkedIn or Facebook, for professional purposes – namely lead generation and customer acquisition/retention.

The term "social" implies that this has been done through means such as personal branding (e.g., including your own blog on your profile), participating in online communities (such as groups) related to particular interests, engaging with others over Twitter discussions etcetera.

A key element here is relationship building; it allows you not only to engage but also interact with potential customers other industry experts who could help you get exposure to the right people.

Social Selling KPIs for Sales Leaders

The latest Social Selling benchmark report provides insights into what companies are doing today, their plans for development over next 12 months, and why/how they measure social selling success.

We highlight which metrics matter most to sales leaders when it comes to measuring effectiveness of company's social media efforts at driving real business results around revenue growth & profitability as well as engagement goals such as lead quality or customer satisfaction metrics.

It also explains how Social Selling is changing sales organisations.

Now, we have to distinguish between KPIs in traditional sales frameworks and KPIs for social selling. A few will overlap, some are irrelevant and some we have to add now.

Irrelevant, traditional KPIs

Traditionally, sales organisations lay great emphasis KPIs such as:

- *Number of dials*

- *Number of calls*

- *and so fourth*

These KPIs are fine for lead generation in traditional sales organisations but Social Selling is not (only and primarily) about generating leads it's all about the quality of those interactions.

The Social selling KPIs should be more focused on user engagement with customers and achieving desired results to measure its success as a Social Selling activity.

A New Set of KPIs

Now, with social selling, these KPIs become obsolete. For a successful campaign, the number of dials are not as relevant as are other KPIs. For example:

- *Number of LinkedIn invites sent*

- *Number of invites accepted*

- *Number of 'touches' (see Account Entry Campaign strategies)*

- *Number of new decision makers added to CRM*

- *Prospect Quality Score rates*

- *Number of meetings booked / calls scheduled*

- *Number of Leads generated coming via social selling campaigns*

- *Revenue generated*

- *Recurring revenue generated*

- *Customer satisfaction rates*

- *Responses per lead source*

- *Social media engagement rate*

These are just examples of Social Selling KPIs.

It is important to consider your Social selling strategy in conjunction with the type of company you are, your field and industry when choosing proper Social Selling metrics that help you measure Social media effectiveness at driving real business results around revenue growth & profitability as well as engagement goals such as lead quality or customer satisfaction for measuring social selling success.

Measuring

Social media is a great way for businesses to connect with their customers. Social networks are important tools that can help you attract new business, develop your brand, and even drive sales.

But how do you know if social networking efforts are paying off?

By knowing what metrics matter most to your company's bottom line - conversion rates, lead quality, etc - brands can build better strategies around measuring their social engagement across various channels.

As a sales leader, you want to identify the top metrics that matter most in your organisation. Studies show that many organisations are measuring these metrics at an executive level but far fewer track them on marketing campaigns. This means brands might not be able to view how successful their efforts have been within certain networks before it is too late. By measuring the right metrics, you can ensure that your social media strategies continue to produce great results.

Technology

Technology plays a crucial role if sales organisations want to measure the results of their social selling strategy. But how do you track and measure activities outside of your own CRM system or technology 'universe'?

Social selling is about creating interest in your products and services or sharing content that will help prospects to become aware of solutions for their problems.

This includes the conversations you have on social networks, but also other channels like forums, emails etc. Social CRM tools are able to give you insights into these different places - enabling your sales team to successfully work with them all. As a result they'll get better visibility into what's happening everywhere customers are interacting online, not only within their own system/platforms where there are often blind spots when it comes down to measuring results.

Social CRM

The more information available at hand provides decision-makers across your organisation with an even deeper understanding of how well certain initiatives drive business value. Social CRM tools can provide you with better insight into what is happening beyond your service desk or walled garden of technology, giving the company a more complete view into how social engagement impacts business results.

The centralised system ensures that all data and metrics are collected in one place. This makes it easy to track progress during campaigns at any stage - from consumer awareness through to conversion rates on purchases made as a result of participating in digital communities like Facebook, LinkedIn etc..

Social CRM systems make it possible for sales teams to see which activities were most effective (e.g., by measuring campaign-specific KPIs) so they'll know where best spend their time going forward. It will even be easier to demonstrate ROI since everything is in one place and easily accessible. Social CRM systems allow you to measure the impact of your social selling activities on revenue generation by measuring KPIs like lead conversions, pipeline value or increased customer loyalty.

Quantifiable Insights for Sales Leaders

This makes it possible for sales leaders to quantify how their teams are performing as well as provide evidence-based justification for initiatives such as training programs, new hires etc.

Social CRMs also make it easier (and less time consuming) to report out across different departments - especially useful if you're part of a cross-functional team that includes members from marketing or PR among other functions. Instead of having each department pull together its own reports and metrics separately, there's now just one source/tool where everything is already collected and measured accurately without duplication.

As LinkedIn has proven to be the leading, and largest, B2B network, sales organisations should have a look at CRM software such as SalesForce or HubSpot, as they integrate seamlessly.

Preparing the strategy as well as the technical landscape for social selling is the foundation for measurable and scalable success.

Conclusion

Social selling is an effective way to generate leads, but it can be challenging due to the complexity of human behaviour and cognition. Strategy design, implementation and measuring results are crucial and require internal teams & management to work hand in hand.

Let's have a look at a high level strategy outline in the next chapter.

High Level Strategy Outline

Social Selling

- *From 'Smile and Dial'*

- *To 'Reach and Teach'*

Aligning Sales & Marketing

- *Dedicated Social Selling Team that sits in-between*

- *Preparing Content Hub tailored to each Decision Maker Persona and their stage in the Sales Funnel*

- *Visualising Sales Funnel*

- *Professional Social Profiles*

- *Campaign specific Email signatures*

Team

- *Identify team members*

- *Clarify responsibilities*

- *Clarify reporting lines*

- *Agree on KPIs*

- *Agree on tracking individual actions*

Account Entry Strategy

- *Identify Accounts*

- *Identify 3-5 decision makers on different levels*

- *Outreach Campaign*

- *Connecting*

- *Engaging*

- *Outreach Email / Phone Call / Voice Messages*

- *Posting relevant information*

- *Creating Campaign Guides for ISRs*

- *Personas*

- *Value Proposition*

- *Call Guide / Sales Script*

- *Email / Voice Message Templates & Guidelines*

Adapting KPIs

- *Number of Invites sent*

- *Number of new connections made*

- *Coding and tracking actions on LinkedIn*

- *Number of new, relevant DMs added to CRM*

- *Number of dials irrelevant*

Requirements

- *Setting up campaign-specific strategy paper w/ timeline, action steps, collateral, etc*

- *Team formation (Who is best suited for this approach)*

- *Identify suitable campaigns*

- *Responsibilities & reporting lines*

- *Identify and define KPI structure*

- *Enabling measuring success factors and tools*

- *Collateral & Marketing Material*

- *Defining Sales Funnel Stages*

- *Defining Personas*

- *Defining Target Accounts*

- *Creating Campaign Guide*

- *Training internally*

Measuring

- *Define and integrate measuring tools such as LinkedIn Social Score, a CRM system, Email tracker, Activity tracker, etc*

- *Define KPIs specifically for Social Selling activities of your ISRs and BDRs*

- *Set targets*

- *Review regularly, especially at the start*

Conclusion

Social selling is a strategy that can be used for account-based marketing sales organisations. social sellers should have the skills to prospect, engage and connect with prospects online in order to drive more leads into your funnel or business.

Social selling also requires social media monitoring of relevant triggers events as well as email follow up campaigns.

Social seller's responsibilities may include preparing content hub tailored to each decision maker persona and their stage in the sales funnel, team formation, identifying suitable campaigns which will require defining personas who should be targeted by specific campaign guides.

Social sellers must also collaborate with sales management and marketing to define a clear social selling strategy that will enable measuring success factors.

Digital prospecting is an effective way for social selling so long as you have the skills required to do it successfully.

Much success!

Josef Reisz

Printed in Great Britain
by Amazon